DESIRE STUDY GUIDE

DESIRE

THE JOURNEY WE MUST TAKE TO FIND *the* LIFE GOD OFFERS

STUDY GUIDE

JOHN ELDREDGE
with CRAIG McCONNELL

THOMAS NELSON
Since 1798

NASHVILLE DALLAS MEXICO CITY RIO DE JANEIRO BEIJING

Published in Nashville, Tennessee. Thomas Nelson is a trademark of Thomas Nelson, Inc.

Thomas Nelson, Inc. titles may be purchased in bulk for educational, business, fund-raising, or sales promotional use. For information, please e-mail SpecialMarkets@ThomasNelson.com.

Scripture quotations, unless otherwise noted, are taken from the HOLY BIBLE, NEW INTERNATIONAL VERSION®. © 1973, 1978, 1984 International Bible Society. Used by permission of Zondervan. All rights reserved. Additional Scripture quotations are taken from the following sources:

(NLT) New Living Translation, Holy Bible. New Living Translation © 1996, 2004 by Tyndale Charitable Trust. Used by permission of Tyndale House Publishers.

(The Message) Scripture taken from *The Message.* © 1993, 1994, 1995, 1996, 2000, 2001, 2002. Used by permission of NavPress Publishing Group.

Desire Study Guide
ISBN: 1-4185-2857-9
ISBN-13: 978-1-4185-2857-7

Printed in the United States of America

07 08 09 10 11 RRD 9 8 7 6 5 4 3 2 1

CONTENTS

Our Heart's Deepest Secret

*It seems to me we can never give up longing and wishing while
we are alive. There are certain things we feel to be beautiful
and good, and we must hunger for them.*
—George Eliot

*As you set out on the first leg of your journey, it might be good to remember
what it was like to begin the first day of exercise, or a new job, or the next
grade level at school in the fall. It felt a little awkward at first, didn't it? It
took time to find your stride. This guidebook will probably feel the same
way. Remember—our desires often seem a secret that may surface at times
and then hide again in the deeper places of our heart. Recalling these defining
desires cannot be rushed, or for that matter, orchestrated. It takes time,
reflection, and allowing your heart to be moved as you sort through things.*

SETTING FORTH

What is the secret set within each of our hearts? (pp. 1–2)

_____

_____

_____

Your existence has a deep meaning. Yet for most of us, it remains hidden, shrouded, buried beneath all the other pressures and demands and busyness of life. But it doesn't go away. Your life has a secret, something written deep in your heart.

What does John mean, "Life comes to us all as a mystery"? (p. 2)

_____

_____

_____

Isn't there a life you have been searching for all your days? You may not always be aware of your search, and there are times when you seem to have abandoned looking altogether. But again and again it returns to us, this yearning that cries out for the life we prize . . . You see, even while we are doing other things, "getting on with life," we still have an eye out for the life we secretly want. When someone seems to have gotten it together we wonder, how did he do it? Maybe if we read the same book, spent time with him, went to his church, things would come together for us as well. You see, we can never entirely give up our quest. (pp. 1, 11)

Is there anything about someone else's life that really looks good to you right now?

_____

_____

_____

_____

WHISPERS OF JOY

The clue as to who we really are and why we are here comes to us through our heart's desire. But it comes in surprising ways, and so often goes unnoticed, or misunderstood.

Unearthing our desire isn't a quick and easy thing. So start with just a good moment from the last few weeks—something that may seem rather simple, but it made you glad.

What happened? Why was it a good moment?

_____

_____

_____

_____

How have other "hints" come to you? What are the movies and music, the people, events, and places that have really stirred your heart over the past few years? Just name them here.

_____

_____

_____

_____

_____

ECHOES FROM THE PAST

What are the two extremes which people tend to go to handle the past? Which do you tend toward? Why?

_____

_____

_____

_____

SHOUTS OF LAMENT

Now for the more difficult side of desire. It's hard for most of us to talk about our losses. But the secret of our hearts is also coming to us even in our greatest losses.

What has been one of your greatest losses or disappointments? Whom or what did you lose, and what did the loss mean to you?

_____

_____

_____

_____

_____

Simone Weil says there are only two things that pierce the human heart . . .

What are they?

_____

_____

_____

Moments we wish would last forever and moments we wish had never begun.

What are we to make of these messengers? How are we to interpret what they are saying? (p. 8)

_____

_____

THE SAME OLD THING

What does John consider the unthinkable symptom of losing Paradise? (p. 9)

_____

_____

_____

How has life turned out differently from the way you thought it would?

_____

_____

_____

_____

Now, what if I told you that life as you now experience it will go on forever just as it is, without improvement of any kind? Your health will stay as it is; your finances will remain as they are, your relationships, your work, all of it. (p. 10)

React to that with as much honesty as you can muster.

_____

_____

_____

_____

_____

_____

IN DEFENSE OF DISCONTENT

What may discontent with our life indicate?

_____

_____

_____

By the grace of God, we cannot quite pull it off. In the quiet moments of the day we sense a nagging within, a discontentment, a hunger for something else. But because we have not solved the riddle of our existence, we assume that something is wrong—not with life, but with us. *Everyone else seems to be getting on with things. What's wrong with me?* We feel guilty about our chronic disappointment. *Why can't I just learn to be happier in my job, in my marriage, in my church, in my group of friends?* (pp. 10–11)

Have you ever felt that—that something is wrong with you, that if you did things better, if you were better, life wouldn't have turned out this way? Do you feel a twinge of guilt about wanting a different life?

_____

_____

_____

_____

What does May say we do with our strong desires for more life?

_____

_____

_____

_____

Jesus was a man of deep desire. It's the secret of his life. Hebrews says it's what sustained him in his darkest hour—that he endured the cross because he so deeply desired what was on the other side, what his sacrifice would accomplish (Hebrews 12:2).

The secret that begins to solve the riddle of our lives is simply this. Life as usual is not the life we truly want. It is not the life we truly need. It is not the life we were made for. If we would only listen to our hearts, to what G. K. Chesterton called our "divine discontent," we would learn the secret of our existence . . . "We have come to the wrong star . . . That is what makes life at once so splendid and so strange. The true happiness is that we *don't* fit. We come from somewhere else. We have lost our way." (pp. 11–12)

What is divine about "discontent"?

_____

_____

_____

Does it begin to make sense of things? You were made to live in Paradise. Put the book down and repeat it to yourself five times: I was made to live in Paradise. What does your heart do with that truth?

_____

_____

_____

_____

Man is so great that his greatness appears even in knowing himself to be miserable. A tree has no sense of its misery. It is true that to know we are miserable is to be miserable; but to know we are miserable is also to be great. Thus all the miseries of man prove his grandeur; they are the miseries of a dignified personage, the miseries of a dethroned monarch . . . What can this incessant craving, and this impotence of attainment mean, unless there was once a happiness belonging to man, of which only the faintest traces remain, in that void which attempts to fill with everything within his reach? (Pascal, Pensées)

What does Pascal say the troubles and woes and heartaches of our lives prove?

_____

_____

_____

_____

_____

Should the king in exile pretend he is happy there? Should he not seek his own country? His miseries are his ally; they urge him on. Let them grow, if need be. But do not forsake the secret of life; do not despise those kingly desires. We abandon the most important journey of our lives when we abandon desire. We leave our hearts by the side of the road and head off in the direction of fitting in, getting by, being productive, what have you . . . If you will look around, you will see that most people have abandoned the journey. They have lost heart. They are camped in places of resignation or indulgence, or trapped in prisons of despair. (pp. 13, 15)

What have you abandoned?

_____

_____

TAKING UP THE QUEST

What does Proverbs 4:23 urge us to do? Why?

_____

_____

_____

_____

Among other things, your heart is the place where your deepest desires come from ("Delight yourself in the LORD and he will give you the desires *of your heart*" [Psalm 37:4, emphasis added]). The way you handle desire is in fact the way you handle your heart.

How have you handled desire in the past?

_____

_____

_____

_____

Striving and indulging—that's how I handled desire for years. Grasping for what I could arrange, denying those desires I couldn't take care of, vacillating from just working hard and using busyness to keep myself from facing my heart to looking for a little something on the side. I have mishandled my desire for years.

—John

We must return to the journey. Wherever we are, whatever we are doing, we must pick up the trail and follow the map that we have at hand. (p. 13)

Of course, you have taken up the journey. That's why you're going through this guidebook. What are you hoping to find?

_____

_____

_____

Do you have any fears about this journey?

_____

_____

_____

And in spite of those fears, how badly do you want to find the life you were meant to live?

_____

_____

_____

_____

THE DILEMMA OF DESIRE

I never knew the dusk could break my heart
So much longing folding in
I'd give years away to have you here
To know I can't lose you again.
—FERNANDO ORTEGA

If it was easy, everybody would be living from desire. We know it isn't going to be easy, either, to really know what it is we desire or to begin to actually live from our heart's desire. There is a fear, a check, a hesitation deep inside all of us. As John ended the last chapter in the book:

Bringing our heart along in our life's journey is the most important mission of our lives—and the hardest . . . Life provides any number of reasons and occasions to abandon desire. Certainly, one of the primary reasons is that it creates for us our deepest dilemmas. To desire something and not to have it—is this not the source of nearly all our pain and sorrow?

In order to move forward, you cannot just pretend that deep hesitation is not there. You must bring up from the depths of your heart your deep ambivalence about desire—and the specific reasons why.

SETTING FORTH

Desire is the source of our most noble aspirations and our deepest sorrows. The pleasure and the pain go together; indeed, they emanate from the same region in our hearts. We cannot live without the yearning, and yet the yearning sets us up for disappointment—sometimes deep and devastating disappointment. (p. 19)

How important is desire to loving others, marriage . . . or singleness? Why?

_____

_____

_____

_____

FRIEND OR FOE?

What desires in your life are feeling like enemies these days—because of the pain they bring or the trouble they get you into?

_____

_____

_____

_____

Can you remember the dreams or desires you had for your life when you were a child? What did you "once upon a time" think you would become?

_____

_____

_____

_____

_____

I do remember . . . trips, adventures, games, reading stories and biographies of the great and good among us. What was once called "pretend" I now understand as yearning as I set myself into the stories of others. Courageous missions of WWII pilots, the adventures of the mountain men taming the West . . . I, too, would accomplish something heroic in my life. Maybe more then than now, I knew there was a reason for me to be here; I was no widget maker. Those grand desires captured me. But somewhere, somehow, they disappeared. Yet even as I recall those more innocent times, there's something inside that seems awakened by the memories. Are they still there?

Yeah, it's embarrassing to say it, but it's true, the desire to be a part of something large, not in size but nobility, to be a part of something heroic is one desire that got lost. Another is to be part of a family in which we see one another's glory, smiling, laughing as we never have, receiving from one another a joy no other circle of people could ever provide. Dear Lord, may it be.

—Craig

WHEN DREAMS DIE

I am not alone in this. Some of you will by this time have lost a parent, a spouse, even a child. Your hopes for your career have not panned out. Your health may have given way. Relationships have turned sour. We all know the dilemma of desire, how awful it feels to open our hearts to joy, only to have grief come in. They go together. We know that. What we don't know is what to do with it, how to live in this world with desire so deep in us and disappointment lurking behind every corner. After we've taken a few arrows, dare we even desire? (p. 23)

What dreams have you had that have seemingly died along the way?

_____

_____

_____

_____

But have they really died? Beneath the ashes of loss, pain, the wasted years and distractions, might there still be a few coals of burning desire? The desire for something more . . . much more?

Are you willing to let them rise and then to embrace them? What do you fear?

_____

_____

_____

_____

Do we form no friendships because our friends might be taken from us? Do we refuse to love because we may be hurt? Do we forsake our dreams because hope has been deferred? To desire is to open our hearts to the possibility of pain; to shut down our hearts is to die altogether.

According to Proverbs 13:12 (NLT), hope deferred does what to our heart?

_____

_____

_____

Like the sea lion, we do settle down and lose desire, but it's rarely a conscious decision; it's more subtle. In fact, the justification makes sense. From within or through others we accept the advice: "Lower your expectations and you'll not be disappointed," or "Your desires are unrealistic," or the dismissing label, "You're a dreamer, a romantic idealist."

What has led you to reduce life to getting on as best you can?

_____

_____

_____

_____

_____

THE BATTLE BETWEEN US

Unrealized, unfulfilled desire has an immense power to shape our lives and relationships. Those things that plague our hearts and souls will have an impact on those around us.

According to James 4:1–2 what is causing many of the relational struggles we face?

_____

_____

_____

Can you see this dynamic of frustrated desire at work in some of your fractured relationships?

Who hasn't come through for you, and how have you battled them as a result? Can you put some words to the specific issues lying beneath. Who blocked whose desire?

_____

_____

_____

_____

THE BEAST WITHIN

There is a reason Jesus chose lust and murder as examples of what happens when desire goes mad within us. He knew what our desperate hearts naturally do when our desires come into conflict. He knew to what lengths we would go to seek satisfaction of our soul's hunger. For the battle of desire rages not only between us, but *within* us. (p. 28)

Paraphrase in your words the dilemma of Paul's life in Romans 7:20–27?

_____

_____

_____

What according to Galatians 5:17 are the two clusters of desires and their origins that cause the battle within?

_____

_____

_____

_____

Describe a recent battle within.

_____

_____

_____

_____

My wife and I were invited to dinner with a couple I simply do not enjoy being with. One set of desires felt strong and went something like this: "Don't go . . . They are 'drainers,' having nothing to offer . . . Are you kidding me? There's nothing in me that wants to spend three boring, miserably superficial hours in conversational cul-de-sacs. I'm not going." The opposing desire, which is easily missed if living on autopilot, seems deeper and truer to who I am and went like this: "I long to touch people's lives and hearts like Christ. This couple, with all their rough quirky edges, are reaching out to us for something. This is an opportunity God may be providing to spend time with them and be available for God to use me in their lives. I'd like to go."

—Craig

There is a nagging awareness inside us, warning that we'd better not feel our hunger too deeply or it will undo us. We might do something crazed, desperate. And so we are caught on the horns of a dilemma; our unmet desires are a source of trouble, and it feels as if it will get worse if we allow ourselves to feel how much we do desire. Not only that, we often don't even know what we desire . . . We try food, tennis, television, or sex, going from one thing to another, never quite finding satisfaction.

Why don't we know what we want? (pp. 29–30)

Dare we awaken our hearts to their true desires? Dare we come alive? Is it better, as the saying goes, to have loved and lost, than never to have loved at all? We're not so sure. After his divorce, a friend's father decided to remain single the rest of his life. As he told his son, "It's easier to stay out than to get out." (p. 30)

What's our dilemma?

_____

_____

_____

Be really honest now: What do you fear will happen if you live fully and freely from desire?

_____

_____

_____

_____

And what will happen to you—to your heart, your life—if you don't live from desire?

_____

_____

_____

_____

DARE WE DESIRE?

Longing is the heart's treasury.
—AUGUSTINE

The last chapter in the book ended with these thoughts:

Our dilemma is this: we can't seem to live with desire, and we can't live without it. In the face of this quandary most people decide to bury the whole question and put as much distance as they can between themselves and their desires. It is a logical and tragic act. The tragedy is increased tenfold when this suicide of soul is committed under the conviction that this is precisely what Christianity recommends. We have never been more mistaken. (p. 30)

SETTING FORTH

Now consider the crippled man at the pool of Bethesda. Put yourself, literally, in his shoes. His entire life has been shaped by his brokenness. All his days he has wanted one thing. Forget riches. Forget fame. Life for this man was captured in one simple, unreachable desire. When the other children ran and played, he sat and watched. When his family stood at the temple to pray, he lay on the ground. Every time he needed to have a drink or to go to the bathroom, someone had to pick him up and take him there.

At what point did he begin to lose hope? First a year, then two went by. Nothing, at least for him. Maybe someone else got a miracle; that would buy him some time. What about after five years with no results?

Ten? How long can we sustain desire against continual disappointment? (p. 34–35)

Where do we all eventually move after continual disappointment?

_____

_____

_____

_____

AN INVITATION TO DESIRE

This may come as a surprise to you: Christianity is not an invitation to become a moral person. It is not a program for getting us in line or for reforming society. It has a powerful effect upon our lives, but when transformation comes, it is always the *aftereffect* of something else, something at the level of our hearts. (p. 35)

What is Christianity an invitation to?

_____

_____

_____

Does that come as a surprise to you? Was that how Christianity was explained to you?

_____

_____

Again and again and again, Jesus takes people back to their desires: "Ask and it will be given to you; seek and you will find; knock and the door will be opened to you" (Matthew 7:7). These are outrageous words, provocative words. *Ask, seek, knock*—these words invite and *arouse* desire. What is it that you *want*? They fall on deaf ears if there is nothing you want, nothing you're looking for, nothing you're hungry enough for to bang on a door over. (p. 38)

Turn the table, and imagine for a moment that you could talk to Jesus about what's on your heart. For that matter, think about your prayers. Do you pray? About what? What have you been asking, seeking, and knocking for?

    Later in the gospel of John, Jesus extends the offer to anyone who realizes that his life just isn't touching his deep desire: "If you are thirsty, come to me! If you believe in me, come and drink! For the Scriptures declare that rivers of living water will flow out from within" (John 7:37–38 NLT). (p. 37)

How have you understood Jesus' offer here—I mean, what goes through your mind when you read this?

LIFE IN ALL ITS FULLNESS

"I have come that they may have life, and have it to the full" (John 10:10 NIV). Not, "I have come to threaten you into line," or "I have come to exhaust you with a long list of demands." Not even, "I have come primarily to forgive you." But simply, *My purpose is to bring you life in all its fullness.* (p. 38)

What does Jesus mean when he says, "I have come that they may have life, and have it to the full"?

_____

_____

_____

_____

GOOD NEWS THAT'S NOT REALLY

Things appear to have come full circle. The promise of life and the invitation to desire have again been lost beneath a pile of religious teachings that put the focus on knowledge and performance . . . Regardless of where you go to church, there is nearly always an unspoken list of what you shouldn't do (tailored to your denomination and culture, but typically rather long) and a list of what you may do (usually much shorter—mostly religious activity that seems totally unrelated to our deepest desires and leaves us only exhausted). And this, we are told, is the good news. Know the right thing; do the right thing. This is life? (pp. 40–41)

Modern day "Pharisees" in the pursuit of sanctification do what with desire?

_____

_____

Christianity has nothing to say to the person who is completely happy with the way things are. Its message is for those who hunger and thirst—for those who desire life as it was meant to be. (p. 43)

What in us is God appealing to in Isaiah 55:1-2?

_____

_____

_____

Describe the life of a godly man as revealed in Psalm 16:11; 42:1-2; 63:1; 73:25.

_____

_____

_____

What news would bring you relief and joy right now? (Don't make it sound "spiritual"—think about your actual life.) (p. 43)

_____

_____

_____

_____

THE STORY OF DESIRE

Have we forgotten—or never been told? Once upon a time, in the beginning of humanity's sojourn on earth, we lived in a garden that was exotic and lush, inviting and full of adventure. It was "the environment for which we were made," as the sea lion was made for the sea. Now, those of you who learned about Eden in Sunday school maybe missed something here. Using flannel graphs to depict Paradise somehow doesn't do it. Picture Maui at sunset with your dearest love. A world of intimacy and beauty and adventure. (pp. 44–45)

Does it ever really crossed your mind that you were meant to live in Paradise—that this life you have is not the "habitat" your heart was designed for—not even close?

_____

_____

_____

_____

Now think about the things that have "turned your head" recently, those things that have roused some hunger within you—even if they merely seemed like "temptation." Can you see in those things your longing for Eden?

_____

_____

_____

_____

_____

All those longings I have for freedom and romance. To travel away to some beautiful place with the Beauty of my life, to linger there for months. Do I need another vacation—maybe to a "better place" this year, somewhere exotic? I may need to get away, but when I think about those longings for escape, I see in them the echoes of what I was meant for. I'm not a freak, I'm not irresponsible . . . I'm just longing for home.

—John

John wrote about the film *Titanic* and why it was such an unprecedented, unparalleled success: Obviously, the film touched a nerve; it tapped into the reservoir of human longing for life . . . [It] begins with romance, a story of passionate love, set within an exciting journey. Those who saw *Titanic* will recall the scene early in the film where the two lovers are standing on the prow of the great ship as it slices through a golden sea into a luscious sunset. Romance, beauty, adventure. Eden. But then tragedy strikes . . . How awful, how haunting are those scenes of the slow but irreversible plunge of the great ocean liner, leaving behind a sea of humanity to freeze to death in the Arctic waters. Everything is gone—the beauty, the romance, the adventure. Paradise is lost. And we know it. More than ever before, we know it . . . The ship has gone down. We are all adrift in the water, hoping to find some wreckage to crawl upon to save ourselves. (p. 45)

And all the hassles and disappointments and deep heartaches of your life—how do you think about those? As bad luck? Probably what you deserved? Something you could have avoided if you'd just done it right? Or do you really see them as the result of living so far from Eden?

_____

_____

_____

_____

_____

_____

_____

But that is not all. The secret of the film's success is found in the final scene. As the camera takes us once more to the bottom of the sea and we are given a last look at the rotting hulk of the once great ship, something happens. The *Titanic* begins to transform before our eyes. Light floods in through the windows. The rust and decay melt away as the pristine beauty of the ship is restored. The doors fly open, and there are all the great hearts of the story, not dead at all, but quite alive and rejoicing. A party is under way; a wedding party. The heroine, dressed in a beautiful white gown, ascends the staircase into the embrace of her lover. Everything is restored. Tragedy does not have the final word. Somehow, beyond all hope, Paradise has been regained. (p. 45)

What's the good news we've been longing for?

_____

_____

_____

And though the *objects* we choose might not be good at all—can you see that the *desire* itself is? The woman at the well's life choices have been a tragic mistake, but the woman at the well's desire for love wasn't evil, was it?

Why did Jesus go after her desire as the more crucial issue?

_____

_____

DESIRE AND GOODNESS

Christianity takes desire seriously, far more seriously than the Stoic or the mere hedonist. Christianity refuses to budge from the fact that man was made for pleasure, that his beginning and his end is a paradise, and that the goal of living is to find Life. Jesus knows the dilemma of desire, and he speaks to it in nearly everything he says. When it comes to the moral question, it is not simply whether we say yes or no to desire, but always what we *do* with desire. (p. 46)

Warning!

So, just to make things clear, I am not saying that every desire that occurs to us is good, nor that we should throw caution to the wind and chase .them all. I'm fully aware that all of us now, so far from Eden, "have desire gone mad within us." Our desire for ecstasy isn't hardwired to God, and we all know it can run in some pretty wild directions.

Are you aware of a desire within you that unsettles you? What are the desires that have historically gotten you into trouble?

_____

_____

_____

_____

Is ecstasy an option for a Christian? Why or why not?

_____

_____

_____

_____

How we handle desire is a deeply moral issue.

In your words what did Jesus say to the morality-equals-good-behavior crowd of his day?

_____

_____

_____

Woe to you, teachers of the law and Pharisees, you hypocrites! You clean the outside of the cup and dish, but inside they are full of greed and self-indulgence. Blind Pharisee! First clean the inside of the cup and dish, and then the outside also will be clean.

Woe to you, teachers of the law and Pharisees, you hypocrites! You are like whitewashed tombs, which look beautiful on the outside but on the inside are full of dead men's bones and everything unclean (Matthew 23:25–27).

How does Jesus feel about the Gospel of Sin Management, the approach to Christianity that focuses on appearing godly from the outside?

_____

_____

_____

_____

Using the parable of the prodigal son, understand that the father represents God the Father, and that the two sons are models of how people handle their desires. The older brother is the picture of the man who has lived his entire life from duty and obligation. When the wayward son returns from his shipwreck of desire, his brother is furious because he gets a party and not a trip behind the barn with the broadside of a paddle. He tells his father that he has been duped; that all these years he hasn't gotten a thing in return for his life of service. The father's reply cuts to the chase: "All that is mine has always been yours." In other words, "You never asked." (p. 48)

Which son are you more like?

_____

The question is not, Dare we desire, but, Dare we *not* desire? (p. 48)

What might your life look like, twenty years from now, if you abandon your heart's desire and take the more conventional road of duty, obligation, and rule keeping? What will it do to your faith?

_____

_____

_____

_____

_____

DISOWNED DESIRE

The danger is that the soul should persuade itself that it is not hungry.
It can only persuade itself of this by lying.
—SIMONE WEIL

We've all abandoned desires that are deep and in this leg of the journey, the
goal is to discover how much of your current life is truly a reflection of your
desires, so that you might begin to live with real faith and genuine hope.

THE DOUBLE-EDGED SWORD

What are the good dangers of recovering desire? What wonderful things might you do?
What might be the effect on other people?

_____

_____

_____

_____

John mentions the lives of King David, the apostles Peter and Paul, and Augustine. In
each case God captures their zeal, their passion and does what with it? (p. 53)

_____

_____

_____

BLESSED ARE THE NICE?

And so Screwtape reveals the enemy's ploy—first make humans flabby, with small passions and desires, then offer a sop to those diminished passions so that their experience is one of contentment. They know nothing of great joy or great sorrow. They are merely *nice*. (p. 53)

"Nice" has become one of the leading virtues in the church today.

What has been the guiding principle or virtue of your Christian life? Maybe another way of asking this is, what have you wanted people to recognize you for?

_____

_____

_____

_____

What is the greatest enemy of holiness? Why? (p. 54)

_____

_____

_____

That whole incident of clearing the temple of the money changers with a whip he had made himself—have you seen that as central to Jesus' personality, or more like an exception to an otherwise very nice guy?

_____

_____

_____

_____

THE MAN WHO WANTED NOTHING

After months of getting nowhere, I asked the obvious: "Gary, why are you a Christian?"

He sat in silence for what must have been five minutes. "I don't know. I guess because it's the right thing to do."

"Is there anything you're hoping to enjoy as a result of your faith?"

"No . . . not really."

"So what is it that you *want*, Gary?"

An even longer silence. I waited patiently. "I don't desire anything." Our sessions ended shortly thereafter, and I felt bad that I was unable to help him. You cannot help someone who doesn't want anything. (p. 56)

Peter said the reason he followed Christ was because Jesus alone had "the words of eternal life" (John 6:68). Is there anything you're hoping to enjoy, a life you are hoping to find as a result of your faith?

_____

_____

_____

_____

_____

What about the King made Elisha so angry?

_____

_____

Is duty or desire the governing force in your life?

_____

PRAYER AS THE LANGUAGE OF DESIRE

What does desire do to our prayers?

_____

_____

_____

_____

_____

Honestly now—how *desperate* are your prayers to God—and how *persistent?*

_____

_____

_____

> Lord . . . I am exposed. I feel like that king Jehoash, the guy Elijah told to
> hit the ground with the arrows—I give it a couple of whacks. Why do I
> hold back in prayer? Why? I can recall only a time or two of loud cries and
> tears . . . but my life is desperate. I am desperate. Oh, God, I am sick of this
> cautious, careful life I lead with you. I AM SICK OF IT. Help me to be
> more honest with you.
>
> —John

Why are we so embarrassed by our desire?

_____

_____

_____

DRIFTING WITHOUT DESIRE

The truth is, I had come to a point where I didn't really know what I wanted in life. My real passion had been the theater, and for a number of years I pursued that dream with great joy. I had my own theater company and loved it. Through a series of events and what felt like betrayals, I had gotten deeply hurt. I left the theater and just went off to find a job. The Washington offer came up, and even though my heart wasn't in it, I let the opinions of people I admired dictate my course. Without a deep and burning desire of our own, we will be ruled by the desires of others. (p. 62)

Without a deep and burning desire of our own, we will be ruled by the desires of others. How long has that been true for you?

Do you feel you're living from your heart in your true calling? Are you closer or farther away than you were, say, five or ten years ago?

And if your life never changes from this point on, if this is what you have to live for the rest of your life—how would you feel about that?

Warning!

Many marriages come to a place where it feels like all duty and no delight. That is a tragic place to wind up, but it is not an excuse to break your most solemn vow ever. Even the worst marriage can be restored to life . . . through the journey of desire.

HOPELESS WITHOUT DESIRE

Why aren't Christians ever asked to give the reason for "the hope that lies within them?" (*1 Peter 3:15*)

No wonder nobody asks. Do *you* want the life of any Christian you know? (p. 64)

What's been the impact of a Christianity without real life hope?

How hopeful would you say you are these days? What are you honestly and truly hoping for? How much anticipation are you living with—a sense that your desires are coming true? (Which is a different question, by the way, than asking, "What would you love to have happen in your life, but you aren't really *expecting* to happen?" Genuine hope has an *anticipation* to it; the other kind is just sort of a passing daydream that we dismiss with a sigh of resignation.)

Warning!

You might begin to feel as if, "OK, so I identify my dreams and desires . . . none of it feels attainable" and then feel tempted to bury them again because of that "it's impossible" kind of feeling. Dear friends, you cannot assess the goodness or the validity of a desire or calling based on the statistical probability of making money at it. The adventure of faith first involves identifying our heart's desire, and then staying with it and with God as he reveals to you how it will unfold. Let him handle the "how." You chase the "what."

FAITH AS DESIRE

What does John point to as the issue in The Parable of Talents? *(pp. 57–59)*

_____

_____

_____

What do you think God thinks about your dreams and desires? More to the point, do you believe he really wants to help you reach them?

_____

_____

_____

_____

What desires over the years have been precious to you, but God seemed indifferent, maybe even hostile to?

_____

_____

_____

_____

_____

What point is being made from the story of the Persistent Widow (Luke 18:1–8)?

_____

_____

_____

_____

The deepest moral issue is always what we, in our heart of hearts, believe about God. And nothing reveals this belief as clearly as what we do with our desire. (p. 59)

What does the way in which you handle desire tell you about your heart's real beliefs about God, and his heart toward you?

_____

_____

_____

_____

_____

_____

MOCKING OUR DESIRE— THE IMPOSTERS

The problem with desire is, you want everything.
—PAUL SIMON

John closed the last chapter in the book by reminding us that when we abandon desire, it doesn't really go away—"it goes underground, to surface somewhere else at some other time . . . The danger of disowning desire is that it sets us up for a fall. We are unable to distinguish real life from a tempting imitation. We are fooled by the impostors. Eventually, we find some means of procuring a taste of the life we were meant for."

The journey of desire involves a two-part repentance all along the way. On the one hand, we repent of refusing to trust God with our desires by allowing them to surface again, allowing ourselves to admit the depths of our desire. On the other hand, we repent by turning from those "other lovers" that we've used to try to fill our desires or at least numb our desires so we don't have to feel them so deeply. This leg of the journey involves some honest reflection on the impostors we've chosen . . . and why.

THE SEARCH CONTINUES

So . . . What is it we're looking for in this life?

_____

_____

_____

LOOKING FOR THE GOLDEN PERSON

What is meant by the Golden Person?

_____

_____

_____

    Titanic roused our desire for Eden, then reaffirmed the leading alternative. It offered romantic love as the answer to the heart's deepest yearnings. The idea is that someone is out there for you, and if you can find him, his love will carry you for a lifetime . . . You don't think you've been immune to all this, do you? Culture has been chanting that mantra for a long time. Of all the films, songs, television shows, musicals, dramas, poetry, and novels you've partaken of in your life, can you name more than five in which human love is *not* held up as the pinnacle of our quest? (pp. 72–73)

Can you? List them here.

_____

_____

_____

_____

_____

_____

Looking beneath the common reasons we marry, what were you looking for when you married? If single, what is it you hope for from marriage someday? If you do not see yourself marrying, what is it that repels you?

_____

_____

_____

Lori was twenty-one; I was twenty-four when we said our vows. They were words, but they were not descriptive of our true intent. We both married to get something. I was willing to give Lori the opportunity to spend the rest of her life filling the voids in mine. Validating me as a man, making my life comfortable, supporting and cheering me on were my expectations. Twelve years later we were in counseling excavating the roots of anger, disappointment, passivity, and fear in our marriage. On our fifteenth wedding anniversary we renewed our vows, wanting to covenant again, knowing now what they truly meant.

—Craig

What is it we hope the Golden Person will give us or do for us?

_____

_____

_____

Why do people "fall" into adultery? What are the "safer" pursuits they make?

_____

_____

_____

Is there or has there been a "golden man" or "golden woman" in your life? What do you hope they will be or provide for you?

Compare the worship given to sex and the golden other that fills nearly every film and song in our culture with the amazing professions of love and devotion to God found in the psalms:

> O God, you are my God,
> earnestly I seek you;
> my soul thirsts for you,
> my body longs for you . . .
> On my bed I remember you;
> I think of you through the watches of the night . . .
> My soul clings to you.
> (Psalm 63:1, 6, 8)
>
> Whom have I in heaven but you?
> And earth has nothing I desire besides you.
> (Psalm 73:25)

Could these words have been drawn from your journal? What's your reaction to these passages?

REACHING FOR THE GOLDEN MOMENT

What is meant by the Golden Moment?

_____

_____

_____

We do the same thing with our hunger for adventure. I imagine there must have been great excitement at the outset for those early explorers— that is, before the mosquitoes and hostile natives became realities. Most of us are not so daring; we prefer our adventure on a more modest scale. Shopping, if you can believe it, has become for most people their experience of a sort of conquest . . . Sport-utility vehicles were the top-selling line in the past ten years, but the irony is that less than 5 percent of them are ever actually taken off road. We want the illusion of adventure without really having to risk it. There is big money in outdoor gear right now; the "look" of the expedition is in. Thirty years ago you wouldn't have found a gym in every strip mall. There, in our air-conditioned sanctuaries, we tone our bodies while watching television. We'll take our adventure *vicariously*, preferring for the most part to be voyeurs of the extreme sport rage or our favorite sports teams. (pp. 76–77)

What modest adventures do you embark upon? What provides the illusion of adventure without really having to risk it? What image are you purchasing and presenting?

_____

_____

_____

What are the two types of idols described? How are they different?

_____

_____

_____

_____

Life stresses us all out, at some point or another. You have a bad day at the office. The kids are driving you crazy. Your checks bounce; your credit card is denied.

When the going gets tough, where do you turn? What gives you some relief from the pressures of your life?

_____

_____

_____

_____

_____

I've had an embarrassing idol, a bag of Cheetos, specifically, extra-crunchy Cheetos. My drive home from church passes a mini-mart (my temple of doom), and many times I've stopped to temper the stress or anxiety I've felt from a day of pastoring. Tough counseling issues or difficult people raise questions about whether or not I have what it takes as a pastor. So, rather than taking the time and doing the heart work of turning to the One True God for the strength, comfort, and guidance I need, I'll reap some level of resolve and comfort by downing a quick and easy "Grab Bag" of Cheetos. And there you have it, a pastor with bright orange lips and fingers "dealing" with the painful realities of life. The momentary relief is soon overwhelmed by the shame, guilt, and embarrassment that I've settled for something so horribly short of what I truly desire.

—Craig

THE NARCOTIC OF PLEASURE

What, often times is the underlying function of pleasure?

_____

_____

_____

How much of your so-called free time is really just an attempt to *numb* yourself from feeling anything? Is TV really enriching your soul? Is overeating really touching your heart's deepest longing? Is straightening the garage or ironing the sheets really necessary?

What function do distractions serve?

_____

_____

_____

THE ASSAULT ON OUR DESIRE

The constant effort to arouse our desire and capture it can be described only as an assault. From the time we get up to the time we go to bed, we are inundated with one underlying message: *it can be done.* The life you are longing for *can* be achieved. Only buy this product, see this movie, drive this car, take this vacation, join this gym, what have you. The only disagreement is over the means, but everyone agrees on the end: we can find life now. (p. 83)

Advertisers know we're looking for the Golden Person, the Golden Moment, the Golden Something that satisfies our quest . . . and they know we'll buy anything, do anything, or go anywhere if we think we might grasp it. Watch an evening of television, paying attention to the commercials. What do the advertisers know about you—and what are they trying to convince you of?

What are the evil one's two basic ploys to kill our desires? (pp. 83–84)

_____

_____

_____

What is the evil one trying to get you to do with your desire these days? Is it working?

_____

_____

_____

OUR TIMING IS OFF

Our commitment to finding life here and now is a commitment nearly all of us share, at a far deeper level than we'd like to admit. There's something just a little hurt and angry in all of us as we find that life is not coming through. (p. 85)

Can you see that demand working in your life? When?

_____

_____

_____

How is our timing off?

_____

_____

_____

_____

Although our desire has taken us to a thousand "other lovers," we must not make a fatal error and try one more time to get rid of it. We cannot revert to killing our hearts. Instead, we must accept the first lesson in the journey of desire: ecstasy is *not* optional. We must have life. The only problem is in our refusal to wait. That is why God must rescue us from the very things we thought would save us. (p. 86)

In some ways, all our work up to this point has been to make that one truth and deep reality written on our hearts: We Must Have Life. Our desire tells us it's true. We cannot live only from a sense of duty and obligation. We cannot live a script written for us by others. We must have life.

Do you see it more clearly now?

_____

_____

THE DIVINE THWARTER

Someone has altered the script.
My lines have been changed . . .
I thought I was writing this play.
—MADELEINE L'ENGLE

Devise your plan. It will be thwarted.
—GOD

The leg you are about to embark on is probably the greatest source of confusion and pain in most people's lives. Why would God make life so hard? Why won't he just grant me what I desire? Why would he actually set himself against the very things that are so precious to me? As Oswald Chambers says, it is here, in the valleys of our lives, that most of us lose heart and give up. That's why it is so important for you to think through these issues.

And as you do, keep this one central truth in mind: God is committed to the healing and the freedom of your heart (Isaiah 61:1–3). He really is for you. When you uncover places of hurt or even a sense of betrayal, hold this truth up as a candle to light your way.

SETTING FORTH

What is it God thwarts?

_____

_____

What is John referring to in his comments about playing chess with God?

_____

_____

_____

CRUEL OR KIND?

This is the point at which God most feels like our enemy. It seems at times that he will go to any length to thwart the very thing we most deeply want. We can't get a job. Our attempt to find a spouse never pans out. The doctors aren't able to help us with our infertility. Isn't this precisely the reason we fear to desire in the first place? Life is hard enough as it is, but to think that God himself is working against us is more than disheartening. As Job cried out, "What do you gain by oppressing me? . . . You hunt me like a lion and display your awesome power against me" (Job 10:3, 16 NLT). (p. 91)

> *Warning!*
>
> *I want to state very clearly that not every trial in our lives is specially arranged for us by God. Much of the heartache we know simply comes from living in a broken world filled with broken people. And we have an enemy in the evil one, who hates us deeply. Jesus warns us that Satan comes against us "to steal and kill and destroy," but that God's overall purpose is to bring us life (John 10:10).*
>
> *Yet there are times when God seems to be set against us. Unless we understand our desperate hearts and our incredible tenacity to arrange for the life we want, events like these will just seem cruel.*

Which of your prayers has God just not answered? What needs or desires has he seemed to ignore? What is your heart's real reaction to that?

_____

_____

_____

_____

_____

_____

What belief about God's heart led Adam and Eve to sin?

_____

_____

_____

Addiction may seem too strong a term to some of you. The woman who is serving so faithfully at church—surely, there's nothing wrong with that. And who can blame the man who stays long at the office to provide for his family? Sure, you may look forward to the next meal more than most people do, and your hobbies can be a nuisance sometimes, but to call any of this an addiction seems to stretch the word a bit too far. (p. 93)

Do you see yourself as an addict? Do you know what your addictions are these days? Or would you describe them in other terms—as "nuisances," or "slipups," or "struggles"?

_____

_____

_____

_____

And on a deeper level, what would feel like death for you to lose in your life right now? What would cause your heart to sink if God told you to give it up?

I have one simple response: give it up. If you don't think you're a chess player, too, then prove it by letting go of the things that provide you with a sense of security, or comfort, or excitement, or relief. You will soon discover the tentacles of attachment deep in your own soul. There will be an anxiousness; you'll begin to think about work or food or golf even more. Withdrawal will set in. If you can make it a week or two out of sheer willpower, you will find a sadness growing in your soul, a deep sense of loss. Lethargy and a lack of motivation follow. (p. 93)

Do it. Give up even those "innocent" pleasures for just one week, and notice what happens. In fact, notice your reaction to my merely *suggesting* you give those pleasures up?

FUTILITY AND FAILURE

What, as a result of Adam's fall is the curse for men?

Both men and women—what's your reaction to this idea of the curse for a man? (p. 94)

Every man knows the reality of the curse because every man must face the ongoing frustration of *futility* and *failure*. No matter how much a man achieves, it is never enough. He has to go out tomorrow and do it all again. If you hit a home run in last week's game, there is such a short time of joy. Next time you're at the plate, everyone expects you to do it again. And again. Futility. (p. 95)

Men—what area in your life really feels futile, like no matter how much you give, you'll never get on top of it?

What does John say is a man's worst fear? (p. 95)

_____

_____

ON THE CURSE FOR WOMEN

What as a result of Adam and Eve's sin is the curse for women?

_____

_____

Both men and women—what's your reaction to this idea of the curse for a woman?

_____

_____

_____

_____

What do you most fear as a woman? What are one or two of the worst things that could happen in your life?

_____

_____

_____

_____

What does John identify as the worst fear for a woman?

_____

_____

_____

And if all this talk of relationships seems untrue for you, let me ask—would you end your life in happiness if you were never, ever really *pursued* as a woman?

THE HARDEST LESSON TO LEARN

God *promises* every man futility and failure; he *guarantees* every woman relational heartache and loneliness. We spend most of our waking hours attempting to end-run the curse. We will fight this truth with all we've got. Sure, other people suffer defeat. Other people face loneliness. But not me. I can beat the odds . . . Isn't there something defensive that rises up in you at the idea that you cannot make life work out? Isn't there something just a little bit stubborn, an inner voice that says, *I can do it?* (pp. 96–97)

Is there?

_____

_____

Can it be done? Why or why not?

_____

_____

_____

_____

_____

This is the second lesson we must learn, and in many ways the hardest to accept. We must have life; we cannot arrange for it. People will avoid this lesson all their days, changing their plans, their jobs, even their mates, rather than facing the truth. "You were wearied by all your ways, but you would not say 'It is hopeless.' You found renewal of your strength, and so you did not faint" (Isaiah 57:10). These are the majority of folks out there, Christian and pagan, who are still giving it a go. Yes, a smaller number have collided against failure and heartache in such a devastating way that they have come to see it can't be done, but they have faded into resignation, or bitterness, or despair. They have taken their revenge on the God who has thwarted them by killing their desire. (pp. 97–98)

What are the three categories of people in this world (and in the church)?
1)

2)

3)

Which do you fall in? Which do your closest family and friends fall in?

_____

_____

_____

"Remember how the LORD your God led you all the way in the desert these forty years, to humble you and to test you in order to know what was in your heart . . . He humbled you, causing you to hunger"

(Deuteronomy 8:2–3). When the Israelites left Egypt, they headed across the Red Sea to Mount Sinai. From there it was only about a two-week journey into the promised land. Fourteen days turned into *forty years*. A blind camel would have found its way sooner than that. (p. 99)

What was the purpose of this season?

_____

_____

_____

_____

Why does God thwart our plans? Why does he seem to take away the heaven we create? Explain.

_____

_____

_____

_____

_____

Many people were shattered by Brent's death. I know I was. Not even on my worst enemies would I wish such pain. But I also know this: the shattering was good. Living apart from God comes naturally; all the striving and arranging is so second nature to me that to have it stopped in its tracks was a great good. I would wake in the morning in those early days of grief, and instead of my desires "rushing at me like a pack of wild animals" as C.S. Lewis said, I knew *it can't be done*. I knew it more deeply and more personally than I had ever known it before. We must learn this lesson, at whatever cost, or the spell will not be broken and we will never discover true hope. (p. 103)

Have you come to the place where you can say, honestly and not just because it's the right thing to say, "God . . . thank you for thwarting me"?

HOPE

Where are we to place our hope? (p. 98)

Hope is everything in sustaining the life of our deep heart. Would you describe yourself as a hopeful person?

"Set your hope *fully* on the grace to be given you when Jesus Christ is revealed" (1 Peter 1:13, emphasis added). I read a passage like this, and I don't know whether to laugh or to cry. Fully? We don't even set our hope *partially* on the life to come. Not really, not in the desires of our hearts. Heaven may be coming. Great. But it's a long way off, and who really knows, so I'm getting what I can now. Our search is limited only by our finances, our options, and our morals. Those with fewer misgivings and greater financial discretion go farther with it. For most Christians, heaven is a backup plan. (pp. 98–99)

To sustain the life of the heart what must we possess?

How often do you think about heaven?

_____

_____

"We are never living, but hoping to live; and whilst we are always preparing to be happy, it is certain, we never shall be so, if we aspire to no other happiness than what can be enjoyed in this life" [Pascal].

What are you looking forward to in the next few months?

_____

_____

_____

What are you looking forward to over the next few years?

_____

_____

_____

_____

What are you looking forward to after your death? (Have you ever written down your thoughts on that before?)

_____

_____

_____

_____

THE GREAT RESTORATION

See! The winter is past;
the rains are over and gone.
Flowers appear on the earth;
the season of singing has come.
—SONG OF SOLOMON 2:11–12

In his letter to the Colossians, the apostle Paul says that our faith and our love actually are rooted in something deeper—in our hope, the hope we have in the fabulous future that is about to be ours (Colossians 1:5). But to be honest, I (Craig) know very, very few people who live with hope. For most people, the future is limited to the next few days or weeks or maybe years. Heaven is either a blank or a weak promise of religious abstractions.

Our hearts cannot live without hope. As John said in The Sacred Romance, hope is to our soul like breathing is to our body. We've got to have it; hope is not optional. Without hope I'm an insatiable hedonist trying to put off the despair circling my perimeter. With hope I am alive, more aware of a "larger story" and more passionate about it capturing my everyday focus (less consumed by my "smaller story"). I find myself more willing to acknowledge the mysteries of suffering and brokenness . . . more accepting that some problems in life are presently unfixable. Hope gives me a context that gives my life a sense of roominess.

In the next three chapters we want your heart to be stunned and surprised at how the life you've always longed for really is the life that God has promised to you.

SETTING FORTH

I was walking in the woods and fields behind our house one evening, four months after Brent's death. My heart was so aware of the loss—not only of Brent, but in some ways, of everything that mattered. I knew that one by one, I would lose everyone I cared about and the life I am still seeking. (p. 107)

What does the thought of being vulnerable to the loss of the people and things that are close to your heart stir in you? Where do these reflections take you? Into anxiety, some level of the blues, or depression, anger, resignation, an awareness and comforting trust in God's goodness?

_____

_____

_____

_____

_____

THE SECRET OF SPRING

Winter tarries long at six thousand feet. Here in the Rocky Mountains, spring comes late and fitfully. (p. 108)

What "winters" of life have you journeyed through already? *Write out some of your recollections from those cold, dark days of pain, loss, resignation, disorientation . . . malaise of heart. If you haven't been through a "winter," what would one look like in your life?*

_____

_____

_____

_____

_____

_____

Going back through previous journals quickly reminded me of one recent bitter winter. Our daughters' adolescence: so many, too many, early mornings I felt the jagged edge of a daughter's scornful dismissing rejection. I wrote then, "How fierce the pain my daughters cause. There seems to be no hope, and worse, no relief. They take all they can, wanting more, scorning our imperfect attempts to engage relationship. We are, to them, Law; we are boundaries; we are limited resources. We are life's cruel limits and consequences. They hate us, as I do." Later: "Right now, it seems to be a severe season with the girls. The poison and venom of a man who insists upon an orderly, pleasant world is being exposed by uncooperative kids." "If she knew how vicious her passive-aggressive adolescence was she would, I hope, fall on her knees and repent of murder." What a cold season it was: "My soul was so distressed with anger, fear, and anxiety yesterday. At one moment I felt as if I was spinning out of control, headed for destruction, certain destruction both in this life and for eternity."

—Craig

What do we believe about winter?

_____

_____

_____

And then, just this afternoon, I rounded the corner into our neighborhood, and suddenly, the world was green again. The bluffs behind our house were transformed. What had been rock and twig and dead mulch was a rich oriental carpet of green. I was shocked, stunned. How did it happen? As if in disbelief, I got out of my car and began to walk through the woods, touching every leaf. Just yesterday the scrub oaks had the twisted, gnarled look of the hands of an old witch. Now they are beautiful, tender, supple like a maiden. The birds are back as well, waking us in the morning with their glad songs. All the chirps and cheeps and whistles and twitters, a raucous melody of simple joy. It happened suddenly. In the twinkling of an eye. (p. 109)

Has spring come for you? Perhaps you are still in a time of winter—what would you hope for spring to bring?

_____

_____

_____

_____

Does life feel more like "winter" than "spring" for you? How does that affect you?

_____

_____

_____

_____

MORE THAN CHURCH FOREVER

But of course we aspire to happiness we can enjoy now. Our hearts have no place else to go. We have made a nothing of eternity. If I told you that your income would triple next year, and that European vacation you've wanted is just around the corner, you'd be excited, hopeful. The future would look promising. It seems possible, *desirable*. But our ideas of heaven, while possible, aren't all that desirable. Whatever it is we think is coming in the next season of our existence, we don't think it is worth getting all that excited about. We make a nothing of eternity by enlarging the significance of this life and by diminishing the reality of what the next life is all about. (pp. 110–11)

At this point in your journey, does heaven excite you? Why . . . or why not?

_____

_____

_____

What would lead you to a deeper excitement about heaven, a longing for eternity?

_____

_____

_____

_____

What's your reaction to the popularly held view that eternity is an unending church service?

_____

_____

_____

_____

Why that reaction?

_____

_____

John says we can only hope for what we desire. Why is that? Describe the Kingdom of God (pp. 112–114).

Does it change your view of heaven to think that what you've written is what will come?

OUR RESTORATION

"Maybe above all [fairy tales] are tales of transformation where all creatures are revealed in the end as what they truly are—the ugly duckling becomes a great white swan, the frog is revealed to be a prince, and the beautiful but wicked queen is unmasked in all her ugliness. They are tales of transformation where the ones who live happily ever after, as by no means everybody does in fairy tales, are transformed into what they have it in them at their best to be." (Frederick Buechner, *Telling the Truth*)

In what ways is the true you different from how you live or how others may perceive you? What do you long to be truly true of you?

_____

_____

_____

> *For a very long time I lived with a well-deserved label . . ."Craig's a comedian." I cannot count the times I've heard, "You missed your calling, you should've been a stand-up comedian." What at one time, for many reasons, I took as a compliment, now causes me to cringe. "Oh Lord," I cry, "you've made me for something grander than being the life of the party, the jokester." As that label fades, a truer, more authentic Craig is unfolding. I believe I am more of a warrior-poet than a "wise" guy/"nice" guy . . . genuinely pastoral, strong, dangerous, truly compassionate.*
>
> *—Craig*

I've spoken with many people who believe that we become "spirits" when we die; that we lose our bodies and float around. Some even believe we become angels. But I don't want to lose my body; I very much want it to be renewed. When we conceive of our future existence as something ghostly, mysterious, completely "other" than anything we've ever known, we place it beyond all hoping for. (You can only hope for what you desire.) (p. 117)

What would you love for your new body to be?

_____

_____

THE EARTH IS RESTORED

In your own words, what will the restoration of the earth involve?

_____

_____

_____

_____

_____

What have we either forgotten or perhaps never been told about the earth's future? (pp. 120, 121–22)

ALL SHALL BE WELL

Our search for the Golden Moment is not a search in vain; not at all. We've only had the timing wrong. We do not know exactly how God will do it, but we do know this: the kingdom of God brings restoration. The only things destroyed are the things outside God's realm—sin, disease, death. But we who are God's children, and the heavens and the earth he has made, will go on. "The wolf will live with the lamb, the leopard will lie down with the goat, the calf and the lion and the yearling together" (Isaiah 11:6). "And Jerusalem will be known as the Desirable Place," the place of the fulfillment of all our desires (Isaiah 62:12 NLT).

It's time to start making some plans for that day.

What would you love to do in the fully restored kingdom of God, as a fully restored man or woman?

_____

_____

_____

_____

THE GRAND AFFAIR

And the people came together, and the people came to dance,
and they danced like a wave upon the sea.
—WILLIAM BUTLER YEATS

Within our hearts we carry many desires. But the deepest of them all is our longing to be loved. Friendship, family, connectedness, understanding, romance, passion—there are many levels and many expressions, but all we have ever really wanted is to be loved. As Gerald May says,

> *There is a desire within each of us, in the deep center of ourselves that we call our heart. We were born with it, it is never completely satisfied, and it never dies. We are often unaware of it, but it is always awake. It is the human desire for love. Every person on this earth yearns to love, to be loved, to know love. Our true identity, our reason for being, is to be found in this desire.* (The Awakened Heart)

But because of the way our lives have gone, we are, all of us, deeply ambivalent about love. This desire has caused us more pain than any other. Loneliness, isolation, misunderstanding, rejection, loss—these are the worst of our heartaches.

And that is why the offer of a life in a community of real love is the most stunning of the promises given to us about our future. To fully appreciate what promise there is for our hearts in the coming kingdom, we must grasp two things—how deeply we want love and what God has promised us in that regard.

THE UNION THAT WE CRAVE

What is it we are looking for in the opposite sex?

Is there another soul to whom a simple glance is all that is necessary to communicate depth of understanding? Do you have someone with whom you can commune in love?

God's design was that the two shall become one flesh. The physical oneness was meant to be the expression of a total interweaving of being. Is it any wonder that we crave this? Our alienation is removed, if only for a moment, and in the paradox of love, we are at the same time known and yet taken beyond ourselves. (p. 135)

There is no union on earth like the consummation of the love between a man and a woman. No other connection reaches as deeply as this oneness was meant to; no other passion is nearly so intense. People don't jump off bridges because they lost a grandparent. If their friend makes another friend, they don't shoot them both. Troy didn't go down in flames because somebody lost a pet. The passion that spousal love evokes is instinctive, irrational, intense, and dare I say, immortal. As the Song says,

> *Love is as strong as death,*
> *its jealousy unyielding as the grave.*
> *It burns like a blazing fire,*
> *like a mighty flame.*
> *Many waters cannot quench love;*
> *rivers cannot wash it away.*
> (Song of Solomon 8:6–7)

Warning!

It's really important in the journey of desire to open up those rooms of longing that many of us closed long ago. As I warned in the chapter, don't let your disappointing experiences cloud your understanding of this. We have grown cynical as a society about whether intimacy is really possible. To the degree that we have abandoned soul-oneness, we have sought out merely sex, physical sex, to ease the pain. But the full union is no longer there; the orgasm comes incomplete; the heart of it has been taken away. Many have been deeply hurt. Sometimes, we must learn from what we have not known, let it teach us what ought to be.

Let me ask you a few questions about this deep longing. For those who are not yet married: *What are you dreaming of in a lover? If your love could be all that you desire, what would that be? Have you seen it portrayed, if only in part, in one of your favorite movies? Describe it here.*

_____

_____

_____

_____

_____

_____

And for those of you who are married, what did you once dream of in a lover? Has the reality matched the longing? If your love could become more of what you want, what would that be?

_____

_____

_____

_____

_____

_____

What does the exotic intimacy described in the Song of Solomon give us a picture of?

_____

_____

_____

OUR LOVE AFFAIR WITH GOD

Small wonder that many people experience sexual passion as their highest transcendence on this earth. This love surpasses all others as the source of the world's most beautiful poetry, art, and music. Lovers reach for the stars to find words fitting enough to express what the beloved means to them and still feel those words fall short. Granted, much of it is hyperbole, expressing more the dream than the reality. But that is precisely my point. This is not merely hormones and sex drives projected outward. It is a clue to a deeper reality, a reach for something that does exist. For this exotic intimacy was given to us as a picture of something else, something truly out of this world . . . After creating this stunning portrait of a total union, the man and woman becoming one, God turns the universe on its head when he tells us that this is what *he* is seeking with *us*. (pp. 129–30)

Is that a new thought to you—that God gave us sex as a picture of something even deeper? What's your reaction to that idea?

_____

_____

_____

_____

_____

_____

_____

We must look back and see the Bible for what it is—the greatest romance ever written. (p. 130)

Is that how you've understood the Bible?

_____

Summarize the story of God's pursuit of his bride.

_____

_____

_____

_____

_____

Does the thought of a deeper, naked intimacy with God entice you? Why . . . or why not?

_____

_____

_____

_____

_____

It does . . . and it unnerves me. In any other relationship I can always hold a few cards close to the chest—not really and fully stand naked before them. I can retain a sense of safety and control. But with God it's different. My fig leaf feels . . . sheer. It feels SO vulnerable. Oh, how I long for a deeper intimacy with God, and yet there are hesitant places in me still. I'll draw close, taste that naked intimacy, then run from it for a while, only to return out of longing. God is gracious with me—far more than I'd be with so fickle a lover. God woos me still, and oh, how I long for the beauty of God. Dearest God, may those turnings away be less, and my stayings with you be longer.

—John

The older Christian wedding vows contained these amazing words: "With my body, I thee worship." Maybe our forefathers weren't so prudish after all; maybe they understood sex far better than we do. To give yourself over to another, passionately and nakedly, to adore them body, soul, and spirit—we know there is something special, even sacramental about sex. It requires trust and abandonment, guided by a wholehearted devotion. What else can this be but worship? (p. 134)

What is your idea of worship? What has been your personal experience of it?

_____

_____

_____

_____

_____

What is God's use of explicitly sexual language to describe faithfulness (and unfaithfulness) to him meant to communicate?

_____

_____

_____

_____

THE SHARED AFFAIR

It is a manifestation of the humility of God that he creates a kingdom so rich in love that he should not be our all, but that others should be precious to us as well. Even in Eden, before the Fall, while Adam walked in Paradise with his God, even then God said, "It is not good for the man to be alone" (Genesis 2:18). He gives to us the joy of community, of family and friends to share in the Sacred Romance. . . . And so our longing for intimacy reaches beyond our "one and only." We come to discover that others mean so very much to us. There is no joy like the joy of reunion because there is no sorrow like the sorrow of separation. To lose those we love and wonder if we shall ever see them again—this is our deepest grief. (p. 139)

Whom have you lost that you would you love to see again, in the life that is yet to come? Who would you hate to leave behind?

_____

_____

_____

I long to see Brent again, and Pop. I pray to see my parents there, young and alive and free. Oh God, I long to know that my wife and sons will be with me. And how I long to see them all in their glory too! How incredible that will be, for us all to know each other as we really and truly were always meant to.

—John

What were Jesus' tears over Lazarus for?

Imagine the stories that we'll hear. And all the questions that shall finally have answers. "What were you thinking when you drove the old Ford out on the ice?" "Did you hear that Betty and Dan got back together? But of course you did—you were probably involved in that, weren't you?" "How come you never told us about your time in the war?" "Did you ever know how much I loved you?" And the answers won't be one-word answers, but story after story, a feast of wonder and laughter and glad tears.

Is there someone whom you'd love to ask a question? A lost friend or family member, perhaps someone from history? What would you ask?

How does John's description of the wedding feast of the Lamb differ from how you've pictured it? (pp. 141–142)Think of some of the best celebrations you've had in your life—great birthdays or Christmases, reunions, intimate dates. Describe a few of them.

_____

_____

So, it would be good to begin to make some plans for that life and those relationships. *Who would you love to spend time with—and what would you love to do together? Take music lessons from Bach? Learn archery from King David? Ask C. S. Lewis for a few more stories from Narnia?*

_____

_____

_____

_____

What hopes has this chapter raised in your heart?

_____

_____

_____

_____

_____

And what does that free you to do with the days ahead of you now?

_____

_____

_____

_____

_____

THE ADVENTURE BEGINS

Enter into the joy of your master.
—JESUS OF NAZARETH

There is one more aspect of our future we must explore if we are to recover heart for the journey of our lives. For though it will be unspeakable joy to live forever in a fully restored universe with the company of the truly intimate, it is not enough. There is something core to our beings and set within our deepest desires that remains untouched. For as the nineteenth-century preacher Thomas Chalmers wrote, one of the "Grand Essentials" of human happiness is having something to do.

Think again about the three great longings of your heart, those deep desires for Beauty, Intimacy, and Adventure. Is your life to come going to involve adventure? If not, how could you be happy there? What about all those gifts and abilities God has placed within you—do those have a future?

Not only is it essential, if we are to live with hope, to know that our future life will be full of creative work and all sorts of adventures, this truth also puts our present life into a whole new light. We are in Training, and a remarkable Promotion is about to be ours. So come and explore more than you ever have: What is it you would love to do?

SETTING FORTH

Some people love what they do. They are the fortunate souls, who have found a way to link what they are truly gifted at (and therefore what brings them joy) with a means of paying the bills. But most of the world merely toils to survive, and no one gets to use his gifts all the time. On top of that, there is the curse of thorns and thistles, the futility that tinges all human efforts at the moment. As a result, we've come to think of work as a result of the Fall. (p. 155)

Do you love what you do for a living? Why . . . or why not?

_____

_____

_____

_____

Do you feel your gifts are being fully used? Do those tasks call out all the potential God set within you?

_____

_____

_____

_____

Is what you're doing now the thing you dreamed of doing when you were a child? What were your dreams for your life's work?

_____

_____

_____

_____

_____

We've somehow overlooked a line in the parable of the talents, a single sentence that speaks volumes about the connection between our present and future life. As you'll recall, the landowner in the story had been away on a journey. In the parallel version told in Luke, the parable of the minas, he was a man of "noble birth" who had gone to "a distant country to have himself appointed king" (Luke 19:11–27). Upon his return, he rewarded those faithful members of his staff in a way that at first seems, well, like no reward at all. "You have been faithful with a few things; I will put you in charge of many things." Luke's version has it this way: "Because you have been trustworthy in a very small matter, take charge of ten cities." This is their bonus—more to do? (p. 146)

What thoughts have you had about God as a rewarder? What kind of a reward do you anticipate? What stirs in your heart with questions such as this? Excitement? Fear? Guilt/shame? Anxiety? Adoration? Hope? Has it felt like a "reward" or something else?

THE JOY OF THE MASTER

How would you describe the God spoken of in Psalm 104:2-3, 10-15; Job 38:12-40 and throughout this section of the book?

What has been the joy of our master?

_____

_____

And what is this "joy" God will share with us?

_____

_____

_____

Although God rested on the seventh day, he hasn't been lying around ever since. Jesus said, "My Father is always at his work to this very day, and I, too, am working" (John 5:17 NIV). For many people this is a new thought—that God is still quite active. Life has led them to believe that he may have gotten things off to a great start, but then he left on vacation or perhaps went to attend to more important matters. But the creative overture recorded in Genesis was only the first movement of a great symphony that has been swelling ever since. The opening notes were not *staccato*, but *sustenuto*, ongoing, unfolding. He's not just sitting around on a throne somewhere. (pp. 147–48)

What have you viewed God as doing with all his "time"? Is this thought of God still working a new thought to you?

_____

_____

_____

_____

_____

The only way to describe God's ongoing creative activity is *extravagant* . . . you don't suppose he experiences his part in running the universe as drudgery, do you?

LITTLE GODS

"So God created man in his own image, in the image of God he created him; male and female he created them." Thus is humanity trumpeted onto the scene, in verse 27 of the first chapter of Genesis. It is a passage familiar to most of us. Too familiar perhaps, for we rarely wonder about what it means. Right here, at the beginning of our existence, is the single phrase our Creator used to characterize us, and most of us haven't the foggiest idea what it implies. (p. 151)

What does it mean that we are image bearers?

_____

_____

_____

Is the thought of having some special work to do in heaven growing on you? Are your thoughts enlarging about what you'll actually do in heaven—that is, in the coming kingdom of God?

_____

_____

_____

_____

_____

What's fairly new is giving thought to heaven! It's amazing really, how long I've gone in my Christian journey without being drawn into many conversations regarding heaven. My thoughts about heaven have been quite simple, generic . . . it's good, it's long . . . I'll be enthralled in the presence of

God . . . and that's been about it. Yes, the thought of having a task, a role, or a part in the ongoingness of heaven is new. My initial concern is that my task would be perfunctory, not really a fit to my desires, my identity (some low-level entry position) . . . I'd hate to be in a heavenly widget factory. In some ways my lack of thought regarding heaven is a reflection of where my focus has been. For most of my life, all my desires were viewed as capable of being filled here on earth (such small desires); heaven really held nothing for me, other than the best alternative to hell.

—Craig

ON MOZART AND MARTHA STEWART

This is precisely what happens when God shares with mankind his own artistic capacity and then sets us down in a paradise of unlimited potential. It is an act of creative *invitation*, like providing Monet with a studio for the summer, stocked full of brushes and oils and empty canvases. Or like giving Mozart full use of an orchestra and a concert hall for an autumn of composing. Or like setting Martha Stewart loose in a gourmet kitchen on a snowy winter weekend, just before the holidays. You needn't provide instructions or motivation; all you have to do is release them to be who they are, and remarkable things will result.

Oh, how we long for this—for a great endeavor that draws upon our every faculty, a great "life's work" that we could throw ourselves into. (p. 153)

So, what is the creative invitation to?

_____

_____

_____

_____

Why is our creative nature essential?

_____

_____

_____

To what degree and where does your life reflect the fact that you are a creative ruler over a dominion?

_____

_____

_____

It's easy to live from an inadequate understanding of what it means to be a "ruler" . . . I've seen and been guilty of the abuse of position and power. I've also made a career out of being passive (though it's never been blatantly obvious). I want nothing to do with either of those models of ruling. My life now seems to be moving in good directions. My desires seem to be more truly concerned with God's plan for others versus my demands of others. I find myself living in the larger story more now, though it still seems very new to me, too new, actually. Several of the "dominions" in which I reflect this creative-ruler dimension of God are: my family (what sway I have over the hearts of my wife and daughters); in my church (Oh, dear Lord, may I, in words and actions, be used to see hearts set free by the beauty and the power of the gospel); among my friends (to love, allow them to love, to share in all the mystery, beauty, and adventures of life together . . . enjoying an authentic communion and God's people). I've lived, and still battle living, in smaller stories. I'm not joking when I say . . . some of the dominions I've ruled over are keeping the garage organized and the spice rack alphabetized.

—Craig

Even if we are loved, it is not enough. We yearn to be *fruitful*, to do something of meaning and value that flows naturally out of the gifts and capacities of our souls. But of course—we were meant to be the kings and queens of the earth.

Dorothy Sayers once wrote, "Work is not, primarily, a thing one does to live, but the thing one lives to do." If only it were so; if only we could land our "dream job," where we'd be paid to do what we love. (p. 155)

THE MONARCHY RESTORED

What future truths does Romans 8:18–19 present?

Christ is not joking when he says that we shall inherit the kingdom prepared for us and shall reign with him forever. We will take the position for which we have been uniquely made and will rule *as he does*—meaning with creativity and power.

Much of the activity of God in our lives is bringing us to the place where he can entrust us with this kind of influence. God takes our training so seriously because he fully intends to promote us. Will it be joy? Does Stephen Hawking enjoy physics? Does Mark McGwire enjoy hitting it out of the park? There are so many ways this "reigning" will be expressed—as unique and varied as there are human souls. God has quite a few "possessions," and it's going to take a lot of looking after by men and women uniquely fitted for the task. (pp. 157–158)

If God is training you, preparing you for a big promotion what purpose lies behind the drama of your life?

_____

_____

_____

Would it have any impact on your life to know now—at least in a sense—what you'll be doing in heaven?

_____

_____

_____

_____

THE GLORIOUS FREEDOM

"Life," as a popular saying goes, "is not a dress rehearsal. Live it to the fullest." What a setup for a loss of heart. No one gets all he desires; no one even comes close. If this is it, we are lost. But what if life is a dress rehearsal? What if the real production is about to begin? As C. S. Lewis wrote in *The Grand Miracle*,

> The miracles that have already happened are, of course, as the Scripture often says, the first fruits of that cosmic summer which is presently coming on. Christ has risen, and so we shall rise. St. Peter for a few seconds walked on the water; and the day will come when there will be a remade universe, infinitely obedient to the will of glorified and obedient men, when we can do all things, when we shall be those gods that we are described as being in Scripture. (pp. 158–59, 160)

What benefit(s) are there in realizing life is a dress rehearsal?

_____

_____

_____

_____

_____

_____

ENTERING MORE DEEPLY INTO DESIRE

Blessed are those who hunger and thirst.
—JESUS OF NAZARETH

And in me wake hope, fear, boundless desire.
—GEORGE MACDONALD

We hope that by now you see why I have spent three chapters trying to bring eternity out of the clouds and into our conscious lives. The dilemma of desire is the deepest dilemma we will ever face. Its dangers are deep and potentially fatal. How, then, shall we not lose heart? If we manage to somehow hang on to our desire, how do we keep from being consumed by it? The secret is known to all of us, though we may have forgotten that we know it. Who wants to fill up with snacks on Thanksgiving Day? Who goes out to buy presents for themselves on Christmas Eve? Is there anyone in his right mind who looked for someone to date at his wedding rehearsal? When we are convinced that something delicious is about to be ours, we are free to live in expectation, and it draws us on in anticipation.

To find the Land of Desire, you must take the Journey of Desire. You can't get there by any other means. If we are to take up the trail and get on with our quest, we've got to get our hearts back . . . which means getting our desire back. And so in this leg of the journey you are seeking a deeper knowledge and understanding of your desire; you are moving forward *by moving* inward.

SETTING FORTH

When I can no more stir my soul to move,
And life is but the ashes of a fire;
When I can but remember that my heart
Once used to live and love, long and aspire—
Oh, be thou then the first, the one thou art;
Be thou the calling, before all answering love,
And in me wake hope, fear, boundless desire.
(George MacDonald, *Diary of an Old Soul*)

Why would MacDonald (writing toward the end of his life, by the way, and not as a reckless young man) pray something as seemingly crazy as this?

_____

_____

_____

_____

What are three things that we must come to terms with in our deep heart? (p. 164)

_____

_____

_____

Over the years of your journey, God will take you back through deeper cycles of learning each of these three "essentials." But for now, how clear are you on each core truth? Are you more deeply aware now how you were made for *life*, and nothing less will do? Are you also aware that despite your best efforts, you cannot arrange for the life you need? And finally, is there a real and growing conviction in your heart that it is coming, life *is* coming to you?

BATTLE AND JOURNEY

Life is now a battle and a journey. As Eugene Peterson reminds us, "We must fight the forces that oppose our becoming whole; we must find our way through difficult and unfamiliar territory to our true home." It's not that there aren't joy and beauty, love and adventure now—there are. The invasion of the kingdom has begun. But life in its fullness has yet to come. So we must take seriously the care of our hearts. We must watch over our desire with a fierce love and vigilance, as if we were protecting our most precious possession. (p. 164)

Is that how you think about your heart these days—as your most precious possession? Does the way you live reflect that conviction?

_____

_____

_____

_____

More and more it is, thank God. Just the other night I was really feeling the pressure to get this project done, finish this journal. But I'd been working on it all day, and my heart was tired. I simply walked away from it, went upstairs, played with my boys for a while, enjoyed dinner with the family, and even then I didn't go back and devote the evening to it. Oh, I felt the demand nagging at me, the strong pull to just go and write, regardless of my weary heart. But I saw it for what it was; I knew the damage it would do. It was good to say no.

—John

So let me say it again: life is now a battle and a journey. This is the truest explanation for what is going on, the only way to rightly understand our experience. Life is not a game of striving and indulgence. It is not a long march of duty and obligation. It is not, as Henry Ford once said, "one damn thing after another." Life is a desperate quest through dangerous country to a destination that is, beyond all our wildest hopes, indescribably good. Only by conceiving of our days in this manner can we find our way safely through. (p. 164)

What words does John use to describe life now?

_____

_____

_____

What two things is life not?

_____

_____

_____

Have you conceived of life—as a "desperate quest through dangerous country to a destination that is, beyond all our wildest hopes, indescribably good"? How have you thought of life?

_____

_____

_____

_____

RECOVERING DESIRE

I continue to be stunned by the level of deadness that most people consider normal and seem to be contented to live with. (p. 165)

Describe Ted in John's story. (p. 165)

_____

_____

_____

_____

_____

If only it were as strong as drink and sex and ambition. We've been bought off by clean socks and television. We'll sell our birthright for a little bit of pleasure and some peace and quiet. I understand. It hasn't taken us long to realize that life is not going to offer what we truly want, and so we've learned to reduce our desires to a more manageable size. (p. 166)

Why are our desires for "the unblushing promises of reward and the staggering nature of the rewards promised in the Gospels" so weak?

_____

_____

_____

_____

_____

Do you think that Jesus would consider your desires too strong, or too weak? Why do you say that?

_____

_____

_____

_____

_____

_____

OUR DEEPEST HEART

Why are many committed Christians wary about getting in touch with their desires? (pp. 166–167)

_____

_____

_____

_____

What two strategies does the enemy use against our living from desire?

_____

_____

_____

_____

_____

For those who have been born of the Spirit and become new creatures in Christ, sin is no longer the truest thing about us. Since the coming of Christ, everything has changed. The joy of the new covenant is the transformation of our deepest being. As Christians, we have a new heart, and that means nothing less than this: our core desires are good. "I will put my law in their minds and write it on their hearts" (Jeremiah 31:33). We don't need to fear recovering our desire because our desire is from God and for God. That is what is most true about us. (p. 168)

What changes as a result of God putting his law in our minds and writing it on our hearts?

_____

_____

_____

_____

The entire future of your Christian life hangs on this promise that you've been given a new heart. Do you believe it? Why . . . or why not?

_____

_____

_____

_____

Yes, we still struggle with sin, with our tendency to kill desire or give our hearts over to false desires. But that is not who and what we truly are. If we really believe the New Covenant, we'll be able to embrace our desire. So, let's come back to the simple question Jesus asks of us all: What do you want? Don't minimize it; don't try to make sure it sounds spiritual; don't worry about whether or not you can obtain it. Just stay with the question until you begin to get an answer. This is the way we keep current with our hearts. (p. 168)

So, how do we keep current with our hearts?

_____

_____

_____

_____

WHAT DO YOU WANT?

Why was Cindy unable to break her addiction to men? (pp. 168–169)

_____

_____

_____

_____

_____

Why would John give up going to church or reading his Bible for a while?

_____

_____

_____

_____

_____

The path to a clearer knowledge of our desire depends on how we've been handling it. Those who have buried desire beneath years of duty and obligation may need to give all that a rest so that their hearts can come to the surface. Abandon all but the most essential duties for a while. You still have to pay the bills, but everything you can jettison, you should. Do nothing unless it reflects your true desire. (p. 169)

Those of you living in the duty camp—what can you give up? The idea might seem impossible or crazy at first. Objections rush to your mind. Your immediate response might be, "Nothing. I don't dare set any of this down." Do you see how bound you are to duty?! We're talking about the survival of your heart here. Of course, you will have to trust God . . . deeply. Let somebody else carry the weight for a while. Or just let it crash. For how long? More than a week. If that sounds too crazy, then how about a three-month break? What will it be?

What counsel does John give to those who have been living to indulge desire?

_____

_____

_____

_____

TEMPTATION

What can we learn about the journey of desire in the story of Jesus' wilderness trial?
(pp. 171–172)

_____

_____

_____

_____

The lie is that the options will bring us what we most deeply want and need. They won't. Every idol is an impostor. Jesus responded, "Those options are not true life." This is the first crucial moment—facing what the options really amount to and realizing "that's not really life." A deep, robust thirst—like we feel after a long, hot hike—can be quenched only by water. To be offered a hot fudge sundae wouldn't tempt us at all. And so we see the importance of entering into desire, of knowing full well what we're craving. (p. 172)

"You don't have to take the route of suffering," [Satan] says. "There are shortcuts. Just give your heart away." It all comes down to worship. What will we give our hearts away to, in return for the promise of life? May says this is "the ultimate invitation to idolatry." Jesus shuts Satan down: "There are no shortcuts, and my heart belongs to God alone."

Once we realize what a precious thing this is, the heart's desire, we must see that to guard it is worth our all. To neglect it is foolishness. To kill it is suicide. To allow it to wander aimlessly, to be trapped by the seductions of the evil one, is disaster. We must be *serious* about our happiness. (p. 174)

What is Satan trying to get you to do with your heart—kill it, or give it away? How will you respond to him?

_____

_____

_____

_____

TUNING THE INSTRUMENT

What's happened to the person who's "lost all sensitivity"? (pp. 175–176)

_____

_____

_____

What's the antidote? In your own words, what is worship?

_____

_____

_____

Back in Mile Eight we looked at how God gave us sex as the metaphor for true worship, for our union and communion with him. That metaphor will be helpful in seeing your way to a deeper intimacy with God. First, there is Courtship.

Where do you find God? What has he used to woo your heart—has it been music? Beauty? Running in the early dawn? Sitting quietly by the window in the night? Lighting a fire in the fireplace and reading a good book?

_____

_____

_____

_____

_____

What has it been for you?

_____

_____

_____

_____

_____

There you have it—go there, regularly, to be courted and to court God.

After a season of Courtship comes Vulnerability. We begin to share our true hearts with God; we open ourselves up to him and share from the depths of our truest self.

What might help you do this? Would it be to journal? Shout? Cry? Bang on the steering wheel? Sing? Pray the psalms?

_____

_____

_____

Do just that, and often.

After Vulnerability comes Communion—just being together, being one. It is the knowing and being known of lovers. Perhaps no words are necessary. Perhaps the words of God's other lovers will help you find a language of your own:

There is nothing created that can fully satisfy my desires. Make me one with You in a sure bond of heavenly love, for You alone are sufficient to Your lover, and without You all things are vain and of no substance.

> *Grant me, O most sweet and loving Jesus, to rest in thee above all creatures, above all health and beauty, above all glory and honor, above all power and dignity, above all knowledge and subtlety, above all riches and arts, above all joy and gladness, above all fame and praise, above all sweetness and comfort, above all hope and promise, above all desert and desire . . .*
>
> *Thou alone art most beautiful and loving, thou alone most noble and glorious above all things, in whom all good things together both perfectly are, and ever have been, and shall be. (Thomas à Kempis) (p. 178)*

LETTING GO

For Jesus I have gladly suffered the loss of all things.
—THE APOSTLE PAUL

This leg may be the most surprising . . . and the hardest. All along John and I have been encouraging you to uncover, discover, recover your heart's desire. We hope that has been going well for you.

Now in this section you must wrestle with the idea of letting go, surrendering your desire to God. When I (Craig) think of "letting go," I focus on what it is I am letting go of. Is it an old refrigerator or my desire for the healing of a close friend's terminal disease? Letting go of an overused fridge is easy; letting go of a friend seems impossible. So to meaningfully speak of "letting go" is to enter the arena of strongly embraced possessions . . . those deeply rooted people and things that define life for us.

In order for your heart to live free, you must learn the spiritual grace of detachment—not abandoning your desire but surrendering your will. You are searching for the secret of hope—which Paul says involves groaning and waiting.

SETTING FORTH

In your own words, how is Paul describing life for a Christian in 2 Corinthians 6:10?

_____

_____

I sat at the intersection staring dumbly at the barriers, the engine idling, cars piling up behind me. God began to speak to my sinking heart: *Your journey lies along another path. You've got to let all that go now.* I knew there was no arguing. I didn't even try to put up a fight. I've been known to plow through his barriers in the past, but not now. Remember checkmate? My grip has loosened in recent years, and I knew this was a call to loosen it even more.

One thing I have come to embrace is this: we have to let it go. (p. 180)

What does the idea of letting go stir in you?

To live in desire is to begin to taste joy indescribable, but much too brief. I (Craig) have had glimpses of life as it was meant to be, but they never last as long as I want. A couple of years ago I was overwhelmed with the beauty of a Southern gentleman's farm. I wrote the following in my journal: "Walking before sunrise, through forest, circling the pond with Colt, the blue-heeler cattle dog, flushing out ducks from the water's edge. What is it about walking through the woods with a dog that's so enjoyable? The beauty of this farm is too much to take in . . . I know this is a once-in-a-lifetime experience, and I want to learn to enjoy it as such. When I see glory I want it to linger, linger in ways it won't (how long does a sunset last, a kiss, a child's smile, a victory . . . not long enough). Don't hold on tight, it won't last . . . let it slip through your fingers." Letting go is losing something and being surprised at what you gain.

—Craig

The more comfortable we are with mystery in our journey, the more rest we will know along the way. (p. 180)

Why must we be comfortable with "mystery" being a part of life?

_____

_____

_____

_____

_____

WILLING TO THIRST

What does living a whole life of longing elicit in you? Paul said he had "learned the secret of being content" (Philippians 4:12), and many Christians assume he no longer experienced the thirst of his soul. But earlier in the same epistle, the old saint said that he had *not* obtained his soul's desire, or "already been made perfect." Quite the contrary. He described himself as pressing on, "straining toward what is ahead" (Philippians 3:12–14). These are not the words of a man who no longer experienced longing because he had arrived. They are the account of a man propelled on his life quest by his desire.

Contentment is not freedom *from* desire, but freedom *of* desire. Being content is not pretending that everything is the way you wish it would be; it is not acting as though you have no wishes. Rather, it is no longer being *ruled* by your desires. (pp. 181–82)

So, in your own words how is Paul, in Philippians 3:12–14, describing the life offered to you?

_____

_____

_____

_____

_____

What did you think contentment was?

_____

_____

_____

_____

What are the three options in living life? (p. 182)

1)

2)

3)

Given those three options how would you describe yourself and how would those who know you well describe you? Why?

_____

_____

_____

_____

Most of the world lives in addiction; most of the church has chosen deadness. The Christian is called to the life of holy longing. But we don't like to stay there. *Why?* God grants us so much of our heart's desire as we delight in him: "You open your hand and satisfy the desires of every living thing" (Psalm 145:16). Not always, not on demand, but certainly more than we deserve. God delights to give good gifts to his beloved. But that old root would have us shift once more from giver to gift and seek our rest through being full. This is the turn we must be vigilant to see, watching over our hearts with loving care. (p. 183)

What good gifts has God given you this past year?

_____

_____

_____

WHAT HOPE FEELS LIKE

We know that the whole creation has been groaning as in the pains of childbirth right up to the present time. Not only so, but we ourselves, who have the firstfruits of the Spirit, groan inwardly as we wait eagerly for our adoption as sons, the redemption of our bodies. For in this hope we were saved. But hope that is seen is no hope at all. Who hopes for what he already has? But if we hope for what we do not yet have, we wait for it patiently. (Romans 8:22–25)

Amazing. Paul is passing along to us the secret of the sojourning heart. We live in hope, and he says hoping is waiting. And groaning. (pp. 184–85)

Here is a simple question to ask yourself to see if you are a pilgrim or an arranger: What are you waiting for? Is there anything you ardently desire that you are doing nothing to secure?

_____

_____

_____

_____

_____

WAITING

To wait is to learn the spiritual grace of *detachment*, the freedom of desire. Not the absence of desire, but desire at rest. (pp. 185–186)

What isn't detachment? What is detachment?

_____

_____

_____

_____

As Thomas à Kempis declared, "Wait a little while, O my soul, wait for the divine promise, and thou shalt have abundance of all good things in heaven." In this posture we discover that, indeed, we are expanded by longing. Something grows in us, a capacity if you will, for life and love and God. I think of Romans 8:24–25(*The Message*): "That is why waiting does not diminish us, any more than waiting diminishes a pregnant mother. We are enlarged in the waiting. We, of course, don't see what is enlarging us. But the longer we wait, the larger we become, and the more joyful our expectancy." There is actually a sweet pain in longing if we will let it draw our hearts homeward. (pp. 186–187)

What do you have a hard time waiting for?

_____

_____

_____

_____

_____

How has "waiting" enlarged you, or, how do you hope or suspect it will?

_____

_____

_____

_____

AND GROANING

How would you define "Groaning"?

_____

_____

_____

How comfortable are you with groaning? Are there any aches you haven't given voice to?

_____

_____

_____

_____

The paradox of grief is that it is healing; it somehow restores our souls, when all the while we thought it would leave us in despair. Control is the enemy; grief is our friend. When the ministry of the

Messiah is described in Isaiah 61, comfort for those who mourn and healing for the brokenhearted are placed at the center of his mission. None of this makes sense until we admit our broken heartedness and give our sorrow a voice in mourning. Only then we will know his comfort. (p. 188)

> Those who sow in tears
> will reap with songs of joy.
> He who goes out weeping,
> carrying seed to sow,
> will return with songs of joy,
> carrying sheaves with him.
> (Psalm 126:5–6)

What comfort is the Messiah offering those who grieve?

_____

_____

_____

What two spiritual disciplines are we encouraged to add to everyday life?

_____

_____

_____

Can you see yourself adding these two disciplines to your life? How?

_____

_____

_____

_____

LET BEAUTY HAVE ITS SAY

As the shock of Brent's death began to wear off, the searing pain of intense grief took its place. It was too difficult to read my Bible. Conversation required more than I was able to give. Frankly, I didn't want to talk to anyone, not even God. The only thing that helped was my wife's flower garden. The solace I found there was like nothing else on earth. I wrote in my journal, *Sitting outside this evening, the Shasta daisies swaying in the gentle breeze on their long stems, the aspens shimmering without light, the full moon rising over the pine crested bluff . . . only beauty speaks what I need to hear. Only beauty helps.*

What pierces the human heart? Why is this so? (p. 191)

What does John mean when he says, beauty heralds the Great Restoration? (p. 192)

SURRENDER

The time has come for us to quit playing chess with God over our lives. We cannot win, but we can delay the victory, dragging on the pain of grasping and the poison of possessing. (pp. 192–193)

What are the two kinds of losses we experience?

_____

_____

_____

What would you count as "losses that came to you" in your life? How did you respond?

_____

_____

_____

_____

Spiritual surrender is not resignation. It is not choosing to no longer care. Nor is it Eastern mysticism, an attempt to get beyond the suffering of this life by going completely numb. As my dear friend Jan describes, "It is surrender *with* desire, or *in* desire." Desire is still present, felt, welcomed even. But the will to secure is made subject to the divine will in an act of abandoned trust. (p. 193)

If you were to let go, where might God take you? Are you willing to go?

_____

_____

_____

KEEPING HEART—
TO THE END

Sometimes I wake, and, lo, I have forgot.
—GEORGE MACDONALD

Well, dear pilgrim, our journey together is nearly at an end. In this last leg that I (John) will provide some guidance for, I want you to consider carefully how you will not lose heart. What will you cling to? What "Rule" will you adopt for your life? What treasures must you hide away? And most important, can you see where the adventure is leading you next . . . and will you follow?

This is preparation for the journey ahead.

OUR WORST ENEMY

Forgetting is no small problem. Of all the enemies our hearts must face, this may be the worst because it is so insidious. Forgetfulness does not come against us like an enemy in full battle formation, banners waving. Nor does it come temptingly, seductively, the lady in red. It works slowly, commonly, unnoticed. (p. 200)

Why is forgetfulness our worst enemy?

_____

_____

_____

_____

Do you wake each morning with a rich and full memory of all God has done and spoken in the past? Or are you like Chuck Colson, who once said that he's an atheist until he has a cup of coffee?

_____

_____

_____

BE FOREWARNED

What was the pattern for the entire history of Israel in the Old Testament?

_____

_____

_____

What have been the cycles of your walk with God over the past six months? Has it been steady, even, ever upward? Or do you fall back into old, abiding places? Describe the cycle.

_____

_____

_____

WHAT WILL WE CLING TO?

In your words, why must we bring the truth into our hearts?

_____

_____

_____

_____

With a recovery of heart and soul taking place in many quarters, my fear now is that we will abandon the pursuit of truth and try to base our journey on our feelings and intuition. "Follow your heart" is becoming a popular message in our culture. Or as Sting sings, "Trust your soul." It will not work. Our spiritual fathers and mothers knew this only too well. In *The Imitation of Christ*, à Kempis warned, "Our own opinion and our own sense do often deceive us, and they discern but little." We must cling to the truth for dear life. (p. 202)

What truths have you been clinging to for dear life? And if the question embarrasses you, if you don't cling to certain truths really that much in your day-to-day life, what does that say about how you are caring for your heart?

_____

_____

_____

_____

_____

That my heart is good—this is the truth I (John) have really been trying to hang with. I have a new heart. My heart is "circumcised to God" (Romans 2:29). Yesterday felt like a breakthrough, like it was finally sinking in. There was a new joyfulness about me and a freedom to speak into the lives of others. Then last night it was brutal battle. Man, it's hard to cling.

—John

What has been the negative affect of the modern era on our understanding of truth?

_____

_____

_____

_____

We have dissected God, and man, and the gospel, and we have thousands, if not millions, of facts—all of it quite dead. It's not that these insights aren't true; it's that they no longer speak. . . . We must return to the Scriptures for the story that it is and stop approaching it as if it is an encyclopedia, looking for "tips and techniques." (pp. 203–204)

What is your approach to the Bible? Does it read like one of your favorite movies—an epic like Braveheart *or* Titanic—*or does it feel like the Yellow Pages?*

_____

_____

_____

_____

Do you come away from your times in Scripture with tips and techniques, duty and information? Or do you find yourself swept up in a Great Drama, "a desperate quest through dangerous country to a destination that is, beyond all our wildest hopes, indescribably good"?

_____

_____

_____

_____

Reminders of the story are everywhere—in films and novels, in children's fairy tales, in the natural world around us, and in the stories of our own lives. In fact, every story or movie or song or poem that has ever stirred your soul is telling you something you need to know about the Sacred Romance. Even nature is crying out to us of God's great heart and the drama that is unfolding. Sunrise and sunset tell the tale every day, remembering Eden's glory, prophesying Eden's return. These are the trumpet calls from the "hid battlements of eternity." We must capture them like precious treasures and hold them close to our hearts. (p. 204)

Has it occurred to you that every movie you love and every song that stirs your heart is telling you about God and the gospel?

_____

_____

_____

Make a list of your favorite stories right now—films, novels, fairy tales. Next to them, write down why you love them.

_____

_____

_____

_____

_____

Now—can you see the themes of the gospel in those stories? Is it a great battle to be fought? Is it a story of undying love? Ask God to reveal to your heart what he has been speaking to you through those very stories.

_____

_____

_____

_____

_____

Let me give you two examples. First is the film The Matrix. *It depicts an entire world held captive to evil—and they don't even know it. Most people assume that the physical world they see is all there is. But that is not all there is. A fierce battle rages for their freedom, and the forces of good are small and brave and spend their lives trying to set the captives free. Finally, the hero, Neo ("the chosen one"), must die in the Matrix to break its power. The whole film is based on the gospel, and a far more powerful and realistic look at the Christian life and mission than you'll encounter most Sunday mornings. The second example is from the film* Gladiator, *also based on the gospel. "A general becomes a slave, a slave becomes a gladiator, a gladiator defies an empire." Isn't Jesus, the Lord of Hosts, the general of angel armies? But when he came to earth he came as a slave, a bondservant. Yet he did not come to bring peace, but a sword, right? And he defies an empire, he pulls down the kingdom of darkness. I love that movie.*

—John

HOW TO CLING

We must be more intentional about holding on to the truth. (p. 205)

Do you have a plan? What will you do to cling to the truth?

_____

_____

_____

_____

How are we kidding ourselves when it comes to keeping heart?

_____

_____

_____

Do you have a rule of spiritual discipline to keep your heart alive and free? Is your communion with God deepening?

_____

_____

_____

_____

What is John's bit of monastic wisdom for contemporary pilgrims?

_____

_____

_____

_____

TREASURES FOR OUR HEARTS

How does journaling help treasure all God has done?

_____

_____

_____

_____

Do you journal regularly? If not, will you begin? Go to a bookstore and find a blank journal that expresses your taste and style. Then set aside several times a week to begin putting down your thoughts, writing out your prayers, capturing the things God is showing you.

If you do journal regularly, how can you enrich the experience? Do you revisit old journals, review what's happened, pick up themes and lessons learned? Another way might be to add photos, pictures from magazines, poems, quotes to your own journaling. Make it a treasury.

At the back [of my journal] there is a section I have entitled "This New Day." There I am writing the central truths I must return to each morning (at least) to guide my desire home. My journal will be filled with all the twists and turns a year can bring, but here is the place I can go for the interpretation of the events and emotions and experiences. Like the Benedictines, we must keep before us the deepest truths— morning, noon, and night. (p. 207)

What are you using to interpret the events of your life, the unfolding drama? Can you make time to do it several times a week?

_____

_____

_____

_____

GOD IS SPEAKING

God is speaking to us more often than we imagine. These are the treasures we must hide in our own hearts—sew them into our jackets if need be—for the dark hours that may come. (pp. 207–208)

Back over the past month or so, what events, conversations, movies, music, Scriptures have stirred you, troubled you, or in some way seemed to be laden with meaning (even if you don't know what the meaning is)? Write them down here.

Then ask God to reveal to you what he is saying through those things. A prayer like this might help:

Oh, Holy Spirit, you have come to lead me into all truth, to reveal to me the things of God (John 16:12–15). You reveal deep and hidden things; you know what lies in darkness, and light dwells with you (Daniel 2:22). Awaken me morning by morning, awaken my ear like one being taught (Isaiah 50:4). Reveal to me what you are speaking through these events in my life. Enable me to hear and understand your voice more clearly. I ask in Jesus' name.

And when he reveals that, write it down.

_____

_____

_____

In your words how does remembering the simple statement "The Story continues" help capture your heart? (pp. 208–209)

_____

_____

_____

_____

Every moment in our lives is like a scene from a movie—every life, for that matter, is like a chapter from a novel. It makes no sense without the rest of the story! Do you see your life as part of a Great Story, a Sacred Romance, a love affair set in the midst of a life-and-death struggle?

What does the phrase, It can't be done, remind us of? (p. 209)

_____

_____

_____

What are the issues in your life that you are still trying to control? Where is it you are still trying to arrange for your little Eden here? What is it you are most deeply having a hard time trusting God with?

_____

_____

_____

_____

_____

_____

Why does the phrase, It is coming, *help? (p. 209)*

_____

_____

_____

_____

Are you living with a deeper awareness that the life you were made for, the secret of your heart, really and truly is coming? What are the remaining doubts? And what stirs your hope that it is true?

_____

_____

_____

_____

Why must we remember that life is Battle and Journey? (p. 210)

_____

_____

_____

_____

What are the latest assaults on your heart? Are you aware of them? How will you live as if you are at war? What will you do to protect your heart?

_____

_____

_____

_____

_____

_____

How does viewing life as a journey help? (p. 210)

_____

_____

_____

_____

Life is now an adventure, and one of the greatest adventures before you is to follow your heart's desire.

What risks do you need to take? What desires need to be pursued? After all the work you've done here, what needs to change about your life?

_____

_____

_____

_____

_____

_____

_____

As you finish this guide book is there a closing prayer you'd like to write out here?

_____

_____

_____

_____

_____

_____